Advanced Level
Essay Writing: German

Advanced Level Essay Writing: German

Eileen Holly

Anne Sansome

Longman

LONGMAN GROUP UK LIMITED,
Longman House, Burnt Mill, Harlow,
Essex CM20 2JE, England
and Associated Companies throughout the world.

First published 1988

Set in 10/12 point Rockwell Light
Produced by Longman Group (F.E.) Ltd
Printed in Hong Kong

ISBN 0 582 35604 0

By the same authors
Alles kapiert?

Preface

We were impressed to read the book 'Advanced Level Essay Writing – French' by Tony Whelpton and Daphne Jenkins, and applaud their enterprise in filling a need for a more careful and structured approach to essay writing at A-level. Their analysis of a possible solution to the task applies to any foreign language, indeed would be useful advice to those writing essays in their mother tongue too. There is a need for the teacher to introduce and practise the skills necessary for a successful essay, as well as a need for the student to realise that time spent on reflection and planning pays enormous dividends. While the basic commentary in this book remains closely allied to its French companion, we have endeavoured to illustrate the points with examples valid for those studying German.

EILEEN HOLLY
ANNE SANSOME

Contents

Chapter 1

What do I have to do?

If you are a candidate for the GCE at Advanced Level in German you have to write an essay in German using from 240 to 400 words on any one of several given subjects.

Length

If you are taking the examination of the Associated Examining Board or the Northern Ireland Board you must write 250 words; for the Oxford and Cambridge Board and the Oxford Board you must write between 250 and 300 words; for the Cambridge Board between 250 and 400 words. The Southern Board requires 350 words, the Joint Matriculation Board 250, the Welsh Board asks for 300 to 350 words and the London Board for 250 words.

There are also Boards which ask you to write longer essays, based on topics you have specially studied. So, your first consideration is the length of your essay. You should become used to counting the number of words you use and you should ensure that you write the number required. Too many, and any excess will not be marked, so that your essay loses its balance. Too few, and you will lose marks from the start.

Choice of subjects

You will be given a choice of five to eight subjects on which to write. Never choose a subject where you are not completely sure of the meaning of the title.

Nature of subject matter

The kind of subject matter varies considerably from Board to Board and from year to year. Some subjects are related to special topics studied by the candidates, but in general the subjects are related to life in the modern world and especially to life in German-speaking countries.

Each of the Boards sets at least one question about politics and the modern world or about some aspect of the social scene such as unemployment, youth or the role of women. Most of the Boards set some kind of general philosophical subject, in which your opinion is asked about such things as the value of work, the speed of modern life, the nature of politeness or the importance of tradition.

Other favourite subjects set concern sport, education or travel. Rather less popular are subjects which require you to invent some kind of imaginative story or to give a straightforward description or narrative of some kind.

Other topics which are set by more than one Board include literature, cinema, television, radio, advertising, industry or technology, work, the future, communications, the police, and war and peace. Controversial subjects like blood sports, zoos and the advantage of one kind of transport over another also appear.

Different ways of setting questions

Short and simple
Sometimes the subject is given in a brief, straightforward and simple way, as for example:
— Tourismus in Österreich.
— Eine Sportveranstaltung.
— Alternative Lebensweisen.

Statements
Often you will be given a longer statement on which you must comment, as for example:
— Die Verantwortung europäischer Länder angesichts der Probleme der Dritten Welt.
— Lernen ist eine Beschäftigung fürs Leben!
— Der deutsche Beitrag zur europäischen Musikszene.
— Die Rolle des Sozialarbeiters angesichts der Probleme der heutigen Gesellschaft.
— Kernenergie in der westlichen Welt.

Questions
Very often you will be asked some kind of question inviting your opinion about a subject, as, for example:
— Ist ein Ausgleich zwischen der westlichen und der sogenannten Dritten Welt möglich?
— Was verstehen Sie unter Bürgerinitiativen?
— Sollten Sportler Amateure bleiben?

— Inwiefern wird unsere Jugend von der 'Popkultur' beeinfluβt?
— Möchten Sie im Ausland wohnen? Wenn ja, wo und warum?

Advantages and disadvantages
Quite often you will be asked to discuss the advantages and disadvantages
of one or more things, as, for example:
— Die Vor- und Nachteile der deutschen Schulwoche.
— Das Für und Wider von Hausaufgaben.
— Was sind die Vor- und Nachteile des Autofahrens?
— Das Für und Wider flexibler Arbeitszeit.

Linking subjects
You may be asked to link two subjects together, as, for example:
— Österreich und der Wintersport.
— Sport und Politik.
— Arbeitslosigkeit und die Gewerkschaften.

Quotations
Sometimes you will be given a well-known saying or a quotation, and you
will be asked to discuss it or give your opinion of it, as, for example:
— 'Reden ist Silber, Schweigen ist Gold.'
— 'Heutzutage suchen viele Arbeitslose überhaupt keine Arbeit mehr.'
  Wie stellen Sie sich zu dieser Behauptung?
— 'Reisen bildet.' Was meinen Sie?

Letters or dialogues
Very occasionally you may be asked to write a letter, as, for example:
— Ein junger Deutscher, der für eine Wohlfahrtsorganisation in Afrika
  arbeitet, beschreibt seinem Freund seine Erlebnisse.
— Eine Brieffreundin in der DDR schreibt ihrem englischen Partner/ihrer
  englischen Partnerin einen Brief, in dem sie ihr tägliches Leben schil-
  dert.

Preparation

As the range of subject matter is so wide and varied, it is essential to do a
great deal of preparation for as many topics as possible.

Firstly, you need plenty of factual knowledge about what is going on in the
world. The best way of obtaining this is by reading as many newspapers,
magazines and books as you can, or by listening to or watching appropriate
radio and television programmes.

Having acquired the essential information about a subject, you also need
to know as much German vocabulary and idiom connected with that subject
as you possibly can.

Finally you must think about all these subjects and try to formulate your opinions about them.

Planning and constructing your essay

Once you have chosen a subject and prepared for it adequately, you must then set about planning a well-constructed essay of the right length.

Your essay will begin with an introduction in which you make clear what your approach to the subject will be. Then there will be two or three paragraphs all closely related to your theme, and finally a proper conclusion.

In the chapters that follow, we shall try to help you plan and write all these different parts of your essay.

Chapter 2

Allow me to introduce ...

The introduction to an essay is extremely important, and yet it is frequently very badly handled, because the writer has often not yet decided what ideas or arguments are going to be used in the main part of the essay. Attempting to write an introduction at this stage is not only pointless, but well nigh impossible. Before you write your introduction, you need to know two things:

a. What is it you are about to introduce?
b. Why exactly are you introducing it?

Making an impression

What, then, is the introduction for? What is it intended to do? Before answering these questions we must answer another: what is the purpose of the essay? The answer can be summed up in two words: to impress. But of course there are a number of ways of impressing which are all relevant to the task of writing essays. We are not thinking simply in terms of gaining high marks in an examination, although we do hope and expect that essays written in an examination will be rewarded in accordance with the impression they make on the reader. We are thinking principally in terms of ensuring that your essay achieves what it sets out to achieve.

Be effective

When you write an essay, you are expressing an opinion or a series of opinions on a particular topic; you are arguing or presenting a particular case; or you are comparing and contrasting two ideas or sets of ideas. It is important to try and make your case or present your arguments as effectively as you possibly can: your aim must be to persuade the reader to accept your argument, or to make the reader better informed after reading your essay and if you are to do this you need all the skill and art you can muster, because you have no right to expect your reader to accept your case if you have not taken care over its preparation. If the argument is not clear, the reader may think either that you haven't thought it out properly, or else that you have made it unclear on purpose in the hope that he or she will be deceived into thinking it is clever. In either case, the discerning reader will reject your argument.

Know what you are talking about

A reader is most likely to be persuaded by an argument that is clearly expressed and easy to follow. But do not think that because something was easy to read it was easy to write too: it is, in fact, harder to write something simple than to write something complicated. (We are not saying that there is something wrong with complexity, merely reminding you that everything complex is made up of a number of simple elements). You need, therefore, to persuade your reader that what you have written is worth reading, and in order to do this, you need to establish, from the very start of your essay, that you know what you are talking about. You need also to present your case in a way that will enable the reader to grasp your argument without having to make an unreasonable amount of effort.

It therefore follows that you cannot write an adequate introduction unless you know exactly what is coming next. There is no point spending time and using up paper and ink warming to your subject. This is a process that should take place in your head, not on paper. Jot down ideas, by all means, but don't be under any illusion that these will constitute a satisfactory introduction if you don't revise them at the end. In fact, there is a very strong case indeed for writing your introduction last.

Take your reader by the hand

So what goes into your introduction? Without a particular essay in mind, that is a very difficult question to answer, so we are going to look at a specific topic. Basically, though, you need to include anything you think is necessary to put the rest of your essay into the most favourable light possible. Does your essay pre-suppose familiarity with certain facts or with a certain way of thinking? If so, give the necessary details as concisely as possible in your introduction. Does your essay involve going step by step through a very close and careful argument? And, since first impressions are always important, use your introduction to make the reader as receptive as possible to the ideas you are about to express. Above all, try and capture your reader's interest. If you don't do that in your introduction, you are not going to do it at all, and in that case your essay will be ineffective and you will have been wasting your time.

Some examples

Imagine that you have been asked to write an essay on the following subject:

Rundfunk oder Fernsehen: Was sind die Vor- und Nachteile?

First, think round the subject (do this even in an examination – do not let yourself be deceived into thinking that time not used for actually writing is time wasted), and make a list of advantages and disadvantages. Then try to assess the relative importance or significance of these points. When you start to do this, you will realise that in fact it depends more on who one is, what your life-style and personal tastes are like, what needs you have, rather than anything in the nature of radio or television in themselves. This could, of course, be your conclusion, but it could also provide you with a useful way of presenting what might otherwise become a boring list of advantages and disadvantages.

A further analysis of the points you want to cover will show that nearly all of them can be put into one of three basic categories: cost, convenience, and entertainment value. There may be several other points which, whilst worth making, do not fit into any of these categories, and would appear rather weak if allowed to stand on their own. Is there perhaps a way of putting these across in the introduction? It is certainly worth considering. Let us look at the points you want to make:

a. *Cost:* A radio certainly costs less than a television as an investment, and you don't have to pay such a large licence fee. Radios are cheap enough for the individual members of the family to own one each, or for a family to have several different types in and around the home.

b. *Convenience:* The radio is smaller, lighter and more portable than a television and can be used almost anywhere. Modern radios with ear-phones don't disturb other people, so the listener can choose his/her own programmes. You can also do other things while listening to the radio, but are restricted when watching TV. TV-sets tend to be installed in one room, which can lead to arguments about which programmes to watch. Yet TV offers an up-to-date pictorial coverage of news and events in a way radio cannot.

c. *Entertainment value:* Socially, TV programmes are a talking point, parti-cularly with certain kinds of programmes such as 'soap operas'. For sheer spectacle, such as state occasions, sport, TV is superior. The visual component can be very exciting, but radio leaves much more to your imagination.

d. *Others:* Radio can cater for longer for specific tastes – pop or classical music, for example.
    You are more likely to be subjected to commercial influences on TV. Local Radio can provide you with important and useful information. Television can be coupled with video, and radio with cassettes. It may

depend on the type of programme as to whether it is better heard only or sound plus pictures.

It would obviously make for a clear-cut, neat presentation to use just the three major categories. There is quite a lot to be said about each of them, so you must watch carefully how you use your word-allocation: you could choose therefore to use the other points in the introduction, being as economical with words as possible, leaving as your conclusion the suggestion that one might weigh up the advantages and disadvantages differently at different times, depending upon one's own requirements and situation at the time.

Your introduction, then, would be something like this:

> Wenn man gern Musik hört, sei es Unterhaltungsmusik, Pop oder klassische Musik, hat ein Radio bestimmt den Vorteil. Will man sich mehr über die Ereignisse in der Umgebung informieren, so kann man sich dem Lokalfunk zuwenden. Möchte man aber nicht nur Ton sondern auch bildliche Darstellungen haben, ist natürlich ein Fernseher unerlässlich. Jedoch bleiben die wichtigsten Aspekte der Frage 'Radio oder Fernseher': Unkosten, Bequemlichkeit und Unterhaltung.

This may not be the introduction you first thought of, but that does not matter; you must never assume that the first idea you have, even if it seems good at the time, is the best possible. Certainly the original idea was good, but not as good as this one, because it would have been more difficult to express in striking terms.

What is it, then, that makes a good introduction? Read it through again and see if you can decide for yourself before reading what we have to say on the subject.

There is a balance in the paragraph: three ideas with a certain rhythm: Wenn man ... Will man ... Möchte man ... It appears that the advantages are all going to be for radio, until the notion of pictures is introduced. This raises the issue of sounds versus images. The paragraph ends with the briefest summary of the points you are going to dwell on in the next part of the essay.

You have made clear the plan you intend to follow. Notice, however, that it is not necessary, when you have listed the points to be discussed, to add 'und wir werden diese Aspekte erwägen': to do so would simply waste words, and, as you will see later, you need all the words you are allowed. In any case, it is much more impressive stylistically to have the three nouns at the focal point of the sentence, and indeed of the paragraph, building up in weightiness and length as well as significance:

Unkosten   Bequemlichkeit   Unterhaltung

Let us look at another topic, this time a more general one:

Der Tourismus in Deutschland.

This title is, in fact, so general that it gives you an immense choice of things to say. Clearly it is better to select and concentrate on two or three ideas than to give a lightning and superficial tour of Germany.

You might want to discuss Germany as a tourist destination for non-Germans, or from the point of view of the Germans' own leisure pursuits. You could differentiate between seasons, between land and water, between countryside and popular resorts, north and south. But whichever way you tackle it, just listing facilities will be boring, so you must decide on the points you are going to stress in the main part of your essay before constructing the introduction. Let us suppose you decide to select aspects of tourism in Germany that attract holiday-makers with particular interests. You might introduce this as follows:

> Warum Deutschland als Reiseziel? Weil das Land Touristen so viel zu bieten hat. Braucht man Ruhe und Entspannung, gibt es Berge und Walder, wo man stundenlang wandern und sich in der frischen Luft erholen kann. Für aktivere Ferien fährt man vielleicht nach Bayern, um den beliebten Wintersport zu genießen. Oder man sucht sich einen der vielen herrlichen Seen aus, um Wassersport zu treiben. Interessiert sich der Tourist für Kultur, so besteht kein Mangel an Museen, Galerien und anderen Sehenswürdigkeiten.

Without repeating yourself you have revealed that you understand that Germany has much to offer, and have selected three features which you can now expand in the rest of your essay. Two sentences: 'Braucht man ...' and 'Interessiert sich der Tourist ...' balance each other in their construction, with a different shape of sentence, 'Für aktivere Ferien ...', between them. You open up possibilities for a conclusion on the lines of incorporating other points not mentioned in the main section of the essay.

Finally, let us look at another topic, which is much more complex:

'Kernkraft: die Energie der Zukunft?'

This is obviously a more controversial topic, and we have deliberately decided to take a controversial, possibly provocative line, even though we do not necessarily subscribe to all the views that we are expressing; you are not obliged, of course, to say what you really feel when you write an essay. This essay is much more complex because there are a number of sub-questions which need to be answered first. To start with, you should explain what is meant by *Kernkraft* and indicate your knowledge of other means of creating power. You may then have to question the value of nuclear power over other sources. If we abandon nuclear power, what happens when oil and coal run out? But what of the environment? What are the dangers of nuclear power, both to those working in the industry, in the locality, or elsewhere, if accidents occur? Suppose they are attacked by terrorists or in war? Are there other not yet developed sources of energy?

These are questions that the main part of the essay will deal with, but you need to give an indication of how you are going to work your way through what could really turn out to be an impenetrable labyrinth if you did not have a guide who knew the way. Here, then, is a possible introduction:

> Ist Kernkraft tatsächlich die Energie der Zukunft? Oder sind die Nachteile so groß, daß man Kernkraftwerke eher abbauen als aufbauen sollte? Sind die Unkosten zu hoch, wenn man an Gesundheit und eine unverschmutzte Umwelt denkt – oder sogar an Leben und Tod? Sollten wir nicht lieber andere Energiequellen suchen, und alternative Methoden entwickeln? Brauchen wir überhaupt so viel Energie? Diese Fragen sind weiterführend.

Notice that although a number of the issues have been raised, no indication has been given of how they are going to be dealt with. It is clear that what is under discussion is extremely complicated, and there is a suggestion of what sort of questions will be discussed before a conclusion is reached. Moreover there is just a hint of the tone or flavour of what is to come, given the use of something as direct as the question 'Brauchen wir überhaupt soviel Energie?' whose main function is to engender a certain amount of interest and anticipation.

Exercises

Here are some essay titles. You are to write an introductory paragraph. Don't forget that you really need to think about the essay and plan it carefully before you write your introduction. For the first three titles we have done some of the thinking for you, and provided a plan. You need to write about sixty or seventy words, not more. Remember that there is not just one way of writing an introduction: it would have been possible to write any number of different introductions for the examples we have given you in this chapter. Just bear in mind that what you are trying to do is gain the reader's attention and persuade him that this is a subject worth thinking about, and that your way of thinking about it is going to be interesting.

1. Sind Sie für oder gegen Boxen als Sportart?
    Main points:
    a. It is a healthy, competitive sport, organized with strict rules.
    b. It is possibly one of the oldest forms of sport, pitting highly trained athletes against one another in single combat. This is exciting and attractive to spectators, who can take sides and identify their favourite.
    c. But is it appropriate to civilised society? Is it not really a primitive form of licensed aggression?
    d. Are we sure it is not harmful to participants and plays to the worst instincts of the spectators?
    e. It also happens to be a sport for men only. Should we encourage such clear discrimination?

2. Was für eine Rolle spielt die Kindergartenerziehung?
   Main points:
   a. It is an opportunity for young children to adapt to social groups outside the family.
   b. It offers young children a chance to learn to share and participate.
   c. Kindergärten provide an introduction to more formal schooling, but with learning through play.
   d. They make available activities not always suitable in the home.
   e. It provides a break for mothers either to have some time alone or to concentrate on other children in the family.

3. Was halten Sie vom Rauchen?
   Main points:
   a. It is a social activity that is relaxing.
   b. Although smoking became commonplace and acceptable, we now know its many dangers.
   c. Smoking is not only dangerous to the smoker but to others too.
   d. It is polluting and also expensive.
   e. Are there commercial interests which do not give way to medical advice?
   f. What of the individual's freedom of choice?

4. Möchten Sie lieber im Ausland leben? Erklären Sie Ihre Antwort.
5. 'Kleider machen Leute'. Stimmt dieses Sprichwort wirklich immer?
6. Sollten Hausfrauen auch Gehalt bekommen?
7. Die Welt im 21. Jahrhundert.

Chapter 3

In conclusion let me say . . .

If, as we suggested in the previous chapter, essay introductions tend to be neglected and rather badly handled, at least the same can be said for conclusions. We read many essays which reach a point where the writers have really said all they want to say, but feel that they need to round off in some way what they have written. There then almost invariably follows a trite, repetitive conclusion, which adds absolutely nothing to what has already been said, and which leaves the reader feeling disappointed and decidedly unimpressed.

Last impressions are important

This is a pity, because if you accept that the object in writing an essay is to impress your reader, for whatever reason, it is clearly against your interests to leave him or her with a sense of anti-climax. Your aim, in fact, must always be to leave the reader thinking: 'Well, that really was very interesting', and feeling that the subject you have been writing about is worth reflecting upon for a little longer.

Do not repeat yourself

It is easier to say what you should not do in a conclusion than to say what you should do, at least until you have a specific example in front of you. Certainly, one thing you should never do is repeat what has been said elsewhere. There are two reasons for this. The first is that if you have something to say in your essay, you must say it as effectively as possible, and if there is any need to remind your reader at the end of what you have said, then you cannot have said it in the first place as effectively as you could or should have done.

The second reason is that, as well as repetition being an admission that you yourself have been ineffective, which is obviously undesirable in a context in which you are seeking to impress, you are also insulting your reader's intelligence, by implying that he or she has not taken in the point you made at the time you first made it. This may not be quite such a fault when you are writing a book, but when you are writing an essay which is probably not much longer than 350 words, no point you have made is ever very far away.

Do not summarise

For the same reason, it is best not to summarise; there is really no point in wasting valuable space. There is a school of thought which says: 'When you are writing an essay, say what you are going to do, do it, then say what you have done'. We do not subscribe to this view, feeling ourselves that it is a pointless and ineffective use of time and effort. If your essay has been written in such a way that your line of thought is clear, there is no need to summarise what you have said; if it has not, then the remedy is to alter the main part of the essay, not your conclusion, to try and put things right.

Know where you are going

We said in the previous chapter that it was impossible to introduce something unless you already knew what it was you were going to introduce. Similarly, it is very difficult to set out on a journey unless you know what your destination is. It follows from this that by deciding what your conclusion is going to be, and roughly what sort of tone it is going to take, by the time you are writing the main part of your essay, you will find the essay easier to write and each point you make will be seen by the reader to be leading clearly towards your conclusion, and will therefore be that much more effective.

What do you put in it?

The answer to this question depends on what kind of essay you are writing, and we hope it will become clearer when you have looked at the examples we are going to give you. As a general rule, though, you will put into your conclusion the answer to the question you have been asked to discuss: if you have not been asked a question, you should put into your conclusion whatever thoughts you feel it is important to leave your reader mulling over. Do not lose sight of the need to impress: what goes into your conclusion must be impressive, because it is the part of the essay that will remain uppermost in your reader's mind, purely and simply because it will be the part of your essay that he or she has most recently read.

Some examples

Let us look again at the essay titles we discussed in the chapter on introductions.

Rundfunk oder Fernsehen: was sind die Vor- und Nachteile?

We said in that chapter that we would put into the conclusion of our essay on this topic the suggestion that you might weigh up the advantages and disadvantages differently at different times, depending on your requirements and situation at the time. Thus our conclusion for this essay would be along these lines:

> Man könnte also sagen, die Wahl Radio oder Fernseher kommt darauf an, was man in seiner Freizeit tun möchte. Das Radio ist ein guter Begleiter zu anderen Beschäftigungen, wogegen ein Fernseher mehr Zeit verlangt, da man nur passiv zusehen kann. Beide aber sind oft nicht nur Zeitvertreiber sondern auch Zeitverschwender. Man ist passiv und nicht kreativ. Andererseits bieten beide Entspannung und auch Anregung.

There is nothing here that repeats what has gone on before, neither is it a summary, yet there is nothing either that comes as a surprise, because we were conscious all the time we were writing the essay that this was going to be our conclusion, and therefore we stated the case in such a way to point the reader in that direction.

Now let us turn to the second topic:

Tourismus in Deutschland.

We began by pointing out that Germany is an attractive tourist venue for people with different interests, whether relaxation, activity or cultural pursuits. The main part of the essay would then be an expansion of these ideas including illustrations of our knowledge of Germany. We now need to conclude, without repetition and possibly bring in points not yet mentioned and add to the dimension of the topic, for we had acknowledged that this is a very general theme that could be handled in a number of ways. Our conclusion, then might be as follows:

> Die Touristenindustrie in Deutschland bietet dem Urlauber Komfort, Unterhaltung und Abwechslung. Ein Aufenthalt in der Bundesrepublik verlockt vielleicht auch zu weiteren Erlebnissen in diesem schönen, vielversprechenden Land. Reisen bildet, so lautet das Sprichwort. Man hat nicht nur die Gelegenheit, das zu tun, was einen unmittelbar interessiert, sondern während man mit Landschaft und Städten vertraut wird, lernt man auch Menschen im Alltag kennen.

Here we have raised two new points: our awareness that tourism is an industry that has to deliver the goods, and that through this industry the

holiday-maker can get a deeper experience than merely fulfilling his im-
mediate interests; 'Reisen bildet' reinforces this latter point. We have set the
matter in a broader context, and we shall say more about this, and about
relevance generally, in the next chapter.

The final topic considered was:

Kernkraft: die Energie der Zukunft?

When we wrote the introduction we gave little indication of the line we were
going to take in this essay, merely posing a number of sub-questions. There
are, of course, a variety of ways in which you could answer those sub-
questions, and your conclusion would depend on your approach. There are,
however, certain possible conclusions you could adopt:

a.   Nuclear power is here to stay.
b.   Nuclear power is a dangerous source of energy that should be avoided
     at all cost.
c.   Nuclear power may be appropriate in some areas where other energy
     sources are not easy to install.

You will have to decide which argument you wish to stress. However both
points a. and b. may be difficult to argue in a way which will convince a
dispassionate and objective reader. You would have to ignore some issues
that would put a contrary view. By choosing c. you are not necessarily failing
to come down on one side or the other: you are showing that your views are
balanced and unprejudiced in a difficult area. We are choosing to illustrate
c., but whichever conclusion you choose, you must make sure that it is one
for which you are going to be able to argue the case convincingly when
you write the main part of your essay. Here, then, is our conclusion:

> Der Entschluβ sich auf atomare Energie zu verlassen, weil sich unsere
> Bodenschätze auch weiterhin verringern, ist nicht leicht zu fassen. Kann
> man den Bau von Kernkraft-Anlagen in dicht bevölkerten Gegenden
> wirklich verantworten? Können Katastrophen ausgeschlossen werden?
> Um uns und unsere Umwelt zu schützen, sollten alternative
> Energiequellen, wie zum Beispiel die Sonne, Wasser und die Gezeiten
> auch weiterhin erforscht und entwickelt werden.

Exercises
At the end of Chapter 2, we asked you to write introductions to a number of
essays, for some of which we gave you skeleton plans. Before writing those
introductions you will have had to think a good deal about the topics
concerned, and therefore will have come to some conclusions. Now look
back at those titles, and write a concluding paragraph to each of the topics
set.

Remember that, as with the introductions, there is no single way of writing a conclusion; the important points are to avoid repetition and summarising, to make sure that what you have written really is a conclusion and, of course, to satisfy yourself that it is a conclusion you are going to be able to justify by the arguments you will produce in the main body of the essay.

Chapter 4

Presenting your case
1: The initial approach

Are you the sort of person who, when presented with an essay question, immediately has a whole torrent of ideas which come flooding into your head, and which then simply need sorting out a little before you write them up into a nice, well-ordered essay? Or are you the kind of person who immediately thinks: 'I know absolutely nothing about this subject, I've no idea what I'm going to write about, and I wish I could have good ideas like everybody else always seems to have'?

The chances are that you are the second type, because most people are, and the impression they have that other people have masses of ideas whilst they have none at all is almost always an illusion. It is true that some people think faster than others; it is also true that some people master more quickly than others the technique of approaching the topics they have to discuss, and eventually become so proficient at it that it appears as if they are missing out some of the stages that others have to go through. But it is, fortunately, a technique that can be learned, and our object in this chapter is to try and help you master that technique, or at the very least get you started along the right road.

Look at the subject

You need a certain amount of information to deal with many of the topics set; it would be extremely difficult, for instance, to write an essay about tourism in Germany if you knew nothing about Germany's geography and attractions. In an examination, of course, you would be able to avoid such a topic, because there is always a good range of topics to choose from. But if you have been given that essay to do at home or in class, your first task is to do some research.

Researching your subject
Before you begin your research, however, you need to do some thinking. It would be a mistake to dash off to the library and read all the books on

tourism in Germany that you can find, because undirected research is wasteful of time and energy, and one of the most important things you can learn is how to work effectively and economically. Before you look at any books at all, you must ask yourself a very basic, but very important question: 'What am I looking for?' In the case of the essay on tourism in Germany let us assume you know nothing about the subject whatever. What, then, is the minimum you need to find out in order to tackle an essay such as this?

a. A basic knowledge of the geography of the country – sea, rivers, mountains and main towns.
b. Some awareness of climatic variations.
c. An outline of transport facilities.
d. Specific appeal of various areas in Germany.
e. Areas catering for particular interests – winter and other sports, walking holidays, cultural activities.
f. Specific events, which attract visitors – for instance, the Oberammergau Passion Play, Oktoberfest, Karneval etc.
g. The effects of tourism on Germany itself.
h. Any problems that may be connected with tourism in Germany.

You will see that the questions asked are not really all that difficult or all that original; you do not have to be a genius to think of questions like these, you simply need to be willing to give the matter some thought and not expect to progress more quickly than you are able. The danger is, though, that you might be afraid of thinking in terms of simple questions like these because you feel that the topic requires a sophisticated, mature answer. If that is the way you feel, rest assured. Everything that looks complicated can be broken down into small, simple elements, and it is a good idea to remind yourself of this every time you begin to write an essay.

Don't be too ambitious

The questions we have suggested above would, in fact, be adequate as a basis for writing a book on German tourism; in that case, though, the answers would be much more detailed than you will need for your essay. The only difference between a book and an essay is one of scope, of depth, of detail. One thing you need to bear in mind the whole time is that you are not writing a book. Consequently the amount of detail you can include is small, and the number of points you are going to be able to make is also small.

Exercise 1
Taking the approach to finding out about tourism in Germany that we have outlined above as your model, work out the questions to which you would need to find answers if you were asked to write essays on the following subjects:

a. Was wissen Sie über die wichtigsten deutschen Feste?
b. Die Rolle der Wasserstraßen in Deutschland.
c. Gastarbeiter im deutschsprachigen Raum.
d. Das Bildungswesen in Deutschland.
e. Ein Interview mit dem Burgermeister eines bayrischen Dorfes: Sie berichten darüber.

Think about it first

The majority of topics on which you are asked to write, however, are ones which do not need any specialized knowledge, but which might oblige you to think about something in a way in which you have not thought about it before. Let us consider another topic:

Sind Gefängnisstrafen immer angebracht?

This topic does not necessarily require more than general knowledge to answer, although there are widely differing views on the subject of crime and punishment. If you think about the question, a number of ideas might occur to you, such as:

a. What is the purpose of imprisonment? Is it to protect the public from criminals, or to take revenge on those who break the law? Is it, or should it be, a combination of both?
b. Is the present form of imprisonment sensible? Does it release prisoners who can take their place usefully in society, or does it make them more hardened criminals?
c. If imprisonment is a form of punishment, is it always effective?
d. Are the prisoners the only ones concerned? What about the effect on their families?
e. Are there other, perhaps better, ways of tackling the problem?
f. Are there improvements that could be made on the present penal system?
g. Should there in fact be harsher punishments for certain crimes?

   There are certainly a lot of other questions you could raise, and we have listed just a few, fairly haphazardly; you could probably add some more to this list yourself. You would then need to think about these things, and sort out your ideas into a logical order. We shall deal with that aspect of planning in the next chapter.

Exercise 2
Look at these topics, and write down a similar list of questions you might ask yourself.

1. 'Es gibt keine schlechten Schüler, nur schlechte Lehrer'.
2. 'Prüfungen sind ein notwendiges Übel'.
3. Werbung im Fernsehen.

You should not find this too difficult if you approach it as follows:

a.   What is the simplest way of looking at this?
b.   Is there more than one way of looking at it?
c.   Have I any personal experience of it?
d.   Is there a conventional way of looking at it, and if so, can one justify adopting the conventional approach?
e.   Do I have any particular difficulty in deciding what line to take on this issue? If so, why? If not, how would I justify my approach to someone who disagreed with me?

With a little practice you will find that you are not really as devoid of ideas as you thought you were, because ideas are simply answers to questions: the important thing is to get used to asking the questions.

Keep to the subject

During the planning stage, which is what we have been talking about, and to which we shall return later, it is important to think all around the subject, and to come up with as many ideas as you possibly can. At this stage you will not be worrying too much about how closely what you are thinking ties in with the subject you are to discuss. But when you come to sift through your ideas and decide what to put into your essay, you need to look very carefully at the exact title you have been given.

You will then probably feel that there are some things you have thought of that do not quite fit in. If that is the case, then however interesting they might be, you must in no circumstances include them in your essay. Never lose sight of the fact that you only have a certain number of words to play with, and in these circumstances digression is unpardonable. It is very important to look at the title again and again, not just when you are starting your essay, but all the time you are writing it. Every time you finish a paragraph, look at what you have just written and ask yourself: 'Is this entirely to the point?' If it is not, you should change it; if you don't, you will have only yourself to blame if you receive a low mark for what you have written. In other words, if you want to do as well as you can, it is better for you to be critical of yourself rather than to leave it to someone else to be critical of you.

Chapter 5

Presenting your case 2: Ordering and paragraphing

When you have thought about the subject in the way we suggested in the previous chapter, you then need to think about the best way of presenting your case. We have already suggested that it is advisable to decide at this stage what your conclusion is to be, and we make no apology for repeating this, because we do feel that it is an important element in ensuring that your case is well put.

The effectiveness of your essay, however, depends just as much on the order in which you present your material and the way your points are balanced. We have already said that if you have some relatively minor points to make, it is better not to inflate them beyond their real importance by giving them a paragraph to themselves: each paragraph must deal with one major point. In fact it is very important that there should be no more than one major point per paragraph.

Restrictions of length

The next thing you must do is establish what the major points are, reducing them to a single sentence at most. At this stage, the order is immaterial. Let us take as an example the points we listed in Exercise 2 of Chapter 2 for the essay:

Was für eine Rolle spielt die Kindergartenerziehung?

The points were:

a. It is an opportunity for young children to adapt to social groups outside the family.
b. It offers children a chance to learn to share and participate.
c. Kindergärten provide an introduction to more formal schooling, but with learning through play.
d. They make possible activities not suitable in the home.
e. It provides a break for the mother, an opportunity to be on her own or to be able to centre her attention on other children in the family.

Next we must count up the number of points we have: in this case five. This means that we have seven paragraphs to write, including introduction and conclusion. Now we divide the maximum number of words we are allowed to write (this is always specified on the examination paper, and it is not advisable to exceed it), by the number of paragraphs. If the result of our calculation is a figure below fifty, we need to think again, because we are trying to put too much into our essay, and we will not be able to present our case effectively enough. The reason for this should be fairly clear; try looking at something fifty words long, and you will see that it is not very much; in actual fact you probably need nearer seventy or even eighty words to be really effective.

Imagine that the Examination Board that set this topic had asked for 300 words, while seven paragraphs require at least 350. We therefore have very little alternative but to reduce the number of points we wish to make. In this case we could do this by combining some of the arguments, such as b. and c., or a. and d. Alternatively you may think that point e. is the least powerful and so decide to omit it, or briefly incorporate it in the conclusion. By reducing the points we are left with:

a.   Meeting others and learning.
b.   Sharing and participating.
c.   Stimulating activities.

This means we have now reduced the number of paragraphs we have to write to five, none of which must exceed a length of sixty words. What we have just said implies that the paragraphs should be of equal length, and we feel that this is important, partly because it ensures that you yourself keep a balance in the way you judge and present your arguments, and partly because it creates an impression of balance, order and careful planning, which are obviously useful if you are trying to make a good impression.

What sort of essay?

Exactly how you go about deciding in what order you should put the points you wish to make depends upon the type of essay, and your first consideration must be to present your material in such a way that your reader can never accuse you of straying into irrelevance.

Compare and contrast
Let us consider the type of essay where you are asked to compare, or compare and contrast, two things, as, for instance, in this example:

Vergleichen Sie das Leben auf dem Land mit dem Leben in der Stadt.

It is tempting in cases like this to deal first with one, then with the other, so that after a paragraph or two about country life you then write about town life, finishing off with the actual comparison, in which you draw out from what you have already written the points they have in common, and in what way they differ from each other.

There are at least two excellent reasons why this is not a good approach. Firstly, if they have any points of resemblance at all (and if you are being asked to compare two things it would be unusual for there to be no point of comparison), you are going to say similar things about each of them, but at different stages in the essay. In other words, you are going to repeat yourself. This is never a good idea, and in this case it is not only totally unnecessary but also wasteful of words in a context where the number of words available is more often than not going to be fewer than you feel you need.

Secondly, you must consider the reaction of your readers. If you use up quite a lot of space telling them about life in the country without any mention of city life, there will inevitably come a moment when they start to think: 'Isn't it about time he started saying something about life in the city?' If that point has been reached, you have lost your audience. It is far better to avoid the risk of doing this by making sure from the very start that each of the matters you have to discuss is mentioned in every paragraph. Thus in one paragraph, you might discuss the question of what there is to do in the evenings, and make your comparison between town and country; in the next you could talk about transportation, and again make the relevant comparison there and then. In other words, tackle it by drawing up a list of matters in which there are resemblances and differences, and deal with each of those matters in turn; you will thus save space as well as making your essay more interesting and effective.

Carrying on a dialogue

Another common type of essay is one where you have to put both sides of an issue, one in which you are discussing some point of view, and there is something to be said on either side. It can be extremely effective if you imagine this as a dialogue between two people of opposing views, so that each point made is countered in the following paragraph by the other point of view. So in the essay in Exercise 3 of Chapter 2:

Was halten Sie vom Rauchen?

you could have something like this:

a. Smoking is a relaxing activity that affords great pleasure to the smoker, especially on social occasions or after a spell of hard work.
b. Yes, but it is very dangerous to health, not only to the smoker but to those around. And it is expensive and messy.
c. If it is so bad, why isn't there a law against it? The government gets a lot of money through tax on tobacco to spend on useful things like schools and hospitals.

d.   You can't expect to destroy the industry overnight. And smokers cost the country money because they often get ill.
e.   But what about the individual's right to decide? There are lots of other dangerous activities, anyway.

You need only to see how much more interesting it is to watch two people arguing with each other on television, putting their arguments and counter-arguments to each other directly, to realise the benefits of this approach. If you imagine a programme in which first one speaker talks for five minutes about why smoking is acceptable, then another speaker talks for five minutes about why it is bad, followed by a commentator who compares what the two speakers have said, you will see the advantages of the approach we are recommending. There is no doubt about it: the dialogue, being more direct, makes for much more compulsive viewing; so it is with essay-writing.

Avoid anti-climax

Whatever type of essay you are writing, there will be some points you want to make which will be more striking than others, and it is because of this that you need to be very careful in deciding in what order you are going to present the points you wish to make. If you start your essay by using your most impressive argument, everything that follows, being by definition less impressive, will seem weak, and your essay will tail off into anti-climax. Your best point, therefore, must come at the end, and the rest must be placed in ascending order of importance. Consider this example. The essay topic is:

Die Gleichberechtigung der Frau: Schon Wirklichkeit oder noch Traum?

You have decided that the following are the points you wish to make and illustrate:
a.   Unquestionably there is now a greater balance between opportunities for men and women than there once was.
b.   There is still a great deal of prejudice against women in certain professions, occupations and activities.
c.   It is important to tackle sex-stereotyping from babyhood onwards.
d.   Men need to be convinced that women should have an equal footing in order to overcome their fears of gross changes in society.

Which of these points you feel is the strongest, is, of course, an individual matter, and it would be possible to write a paragraph on each of them which would make it seem a very significant point. But if you feel strongly that women are most discriminated against in the job market, point b., then you are likely to express that in a more effective way than a point which you feel is less significant. In this case you might choose the order of points as b., c., d., a.

You might wish to concentrate on point a., and imply that female emancipation has been largely achieved, dealing with positive rather than negative aspects. It is important to see the way the various point are expressed to determine what the writer feels is the most telling argument. In this case, you could keep the order of points as listed.

The weakness or strength of these and other points is naturally relative, and if any of your points is really weak, it is not worth making at all, and you would do better to leave it out and use the extra word-availability for more important points; but you must aim to write each paragraph in such a way as to put the weakest of your points in the best possible light.

Exercises

Each of the essay topics given below is followed by a list of points which might be introduced in an essay on that topic. But they have been listed haphazardly, and in many cases expressed in such a way that the full possibilities of the point to be made may not be immediately obvious. Look at these in the light of what we have just been saying, and in the light of the length of the essay you are expected to write, and decide:

a.   whether you need to discard any, and if so which;
b.   whether you would like to add a point or points of your own, and if so, what;
c.   what are the possibilities of each of the points you are keeping;
d.   whether any of the points would be better put in the introduction or the conclusion;
e.   in what order it would be best to deal with them, and why.

1.   Die Vor- und Nachteile des deutschen Schultags.   (250 words maximum)

    a.   School on Saturday.
    b.   Early start – early finish.
    c.   Free afternoons.
    d.   More subjects studied for longer.
    e.   Less sport.
    f.   Lots of homework and tests.

2.   Sollten Privatschulen in Ihrem Land abgeschafft werden?
                          (350 words maximum)

    a.   More individual attention.
    b.   Good sports facilities.
    c.   In the case of boarding schools, children would be happier at home.
    d.   A system that benefits the rich and gives them privileges.
    e.   Maintains old traditions.
    f.   Parents' freedom to choose the type of education for their children.
    g.   Upholds high academic standards.
    h.   Resources should go into state schools.
    i.   Discipline and routine are good training.

3. Sollte man Polizisten bewaffnen oder nicht?   (300 words maximum)

   a. Easier to exercise control.
   b. Strengthens the policeman's authority.
   c. Danger of shooting at wrong targets.
   d. Violence can lead to violence.
   e. Needed to counteract increasing violence in society.
   f. Not necessary to many police duties.
   g. Expensive in training and equipment.
   h. Less dangerous techniques are available.
   i. May lead to more sophisticated crime.
   j. Protects the policeman and the public.

4. Wie wichtig ist der Wintersport?   (300 words maximum)

   a. Holiday activities.
   b. Provides lots of jobs in the area.
   c. Encourages healthy activity.
   d. Fosters competitive sport.
   e. Encourages a whole industry of clothes, equipment etc.
   f. Using natural settings to advantage.
   g. Not available to all because of cost.
   h. Can be dangerous.
   i. Social life in resorts.
   j. Entertainment via television.

5. Was sollte man in Betracht ziehen, wenn man einen Lebenspartner wählt?   (300 words maximum)

   a. Good cook/handy about the house.
   b. Physically attractive.
   c. Independent/self-sufficient.
   d. Sociable.
   e. Fond of children.
   f. Easy-going nature.
   g. Good conversation.
   h. Intelligent.

Chapter 6
Let's start writing

Up to this point we have been concerned solely with the marshalling of your ideas, the object being to arrange them in such a way that your reader will be suitably impressed by the content of your essay. The way you express these ideas is equally important, of course, because it is perfectly possible for a well thought-out essay to compensate to a certain extent for lack of solid argument, but not entirely. What we should be aiming for is, naturally, an essay which is both well thought-out and well written.

Be accurate

The first thing you have to make sure of is that what you are writing is correct German. There is no point in trying to achieve an effect with the strength of your argument or the brilliance of your style if your strong verbs are incorrect, if your adjective endings are carelessly written, or if your German doesn't make sense to a native German speaker. This, however, is your concern; the only person who can improve the accuracy of your written German is you yourself and you should bear in mind that in examinations it is accuracy that carries the most weight. It doesn't matter how brilliant your thinking is; if your essay is full of grammatical mistakes, you will fail. It must also be said, though, that you will not get a very high mark if you do not display clarity of thought and clarity of expression.

However, even though you may have a good mastery of grammar, it is always possible to make careless mistakes and thus be penalised; all the more so under the stress of examination conditions. It may therefore help you to make a check-list of grammatical points which you can use when reading over your work. These might include such points as: word order; verbs – tenses, singular/plural, strong or weak, governing particular cases; gender; case; adjective endings; pronouns; punctuation and spelling.

Don't think in English

It is very tempting when you are still in the comparatively early stages of learning a foreign language to think out what you want to say in English first. If you are lucky, you will already have been discouraged from doing this, and if you took note of that discouragement and acted upon it, so much the better. Whatever you have done in the past, though, it is absolutely essential that you get into the habit *now* of thinking straight away of German expressions you are going to use in your essay, for two very good reasons:

a. if you think the essay out in English first the reader can always tell;
b. if you don't make a start on trying to think in German now, you will never be able to do it.

The worst thing you can do, though, (and there is no shortage of candidates doing this at A Level) is to think out sentences in what one might call debating-style language, which you then try to translate into German. Given that translation from English into German is very demanding anyway, and that doing it that way imposes a restriction on you that even the examiners think it would be unreasonable to impose, this is not a very useful approach. The fact is that you have already learnt a lot of expressions that you know are good German, and as time goes you will learn many more. What is important first of all is that as you learn such expressions you must use them; over and over again, until they really become part of the armoury of language that you are actively able to use. There will inevitably be a transitional stage, during which you will have some ideas in English and some in German, but eventually, if you persevere, you will find that you have achieved what you hoped to achieve, and have started to write in German without thinking in English at all.

Beware of clichés

One thing to beware of though is learning expressions which you then try to bring into your essay whether they are appropriate or not; in particular you should only use sparingly such expressions as you have learned, and when you do use them, make sure you use them intelligently. An example of foolish usage would be:

> Meiner Meinung nach ist dies im großen und ganzen eine umstrittene Frage, die schwer zu lösen ist; schließlich und endlich konnte man sagen, daß es Vorteile sowie Nachteile gibt.

None of the parts of this sentence is grammatically inaccurate, but the fact is that it both uses up a lot of words without actually saying anything, and that it does nothing to create a good impression of the writer's clear thinking and ability to put down ideas.

Constructive reading

What you really need to do to help you to prepare your essays is to read – and always with a pencil and paper nearby. Read, in particular, articles from newspapers and magazines, making sure they are recent issues, and not several years old. Newspapers like the *Frankfurter Allgemeine* and the *Süddeutsche Zeitung*, and magazines like *Spiegel* and *Stern* are excellent sources of material, as is *Jugendscala*, which is available free to schools. Remember that these articles are really nothing more than essays by journalists. Go through these regularly, making a note of any expression that strikes you as being one you could usefully add to your store, then use it at the first available opportunity. This has three advantages over learning something from a book:

a.   you have made the choice yourself, and that fact alone means that you will be more likely to be able to assimilate it naturally into your normal style of writing;

b.   if you are using really recent issues, you will be much more up to date than any book can be;

c.   it is easier to learn by reading short passages on a variety of topics than to concentrate on one topic treated at length in a book.

Style

What we are really saying is that you need to develop your own particular and personal style, but before we get down to that, it would perhaps be advisable to consider for a moment what style is.

What is style?

We have already made it clear that whatever you write, you are trying to achieve an effect: the poet may be trying to move you to tears; the novelist may be trying to get you to identify with his hero or heroine; the newspaper leader-writer may be trying to win you over to his way of thinking. But whatever they are trying to do, they endeavour to write in such a way that they achieve their ends without the reader really being aware that it is the way the writer has written, rather than what he has written, that has affected him. That is style.

What, then, is good style? It is not necessarily very fine writing; it is not a way of expressing yourself which the reader stands back and admires as he reads it. That is more likely to the bad style, unless, of course, you are deliberately looking at the way it is written, as you do when you are studying literature. Good style is purely and simply a way of writing which ensures that you achieve what you set out to achieve. Bad style is anything which stands in the way. If, as you are reading something, you stop and think about the way it is written rather than about the thoughts or feelings which are being expressed, there is something wrong with the way it is written. That is why the example given earlier of the paragraph containing one cliché after another was bad style: because if the reader says to himself 'this is just a mass of clichés', then you are not going to achieve your aim.

Say what you mean

Apart from making sure that what you have written is accurate as far as the German is concerned, you should also ensure that it makes sense, which is not necessarily the same thing.

Think over carefully what you have written. Supposing you had included the following sentence in an essay on the subject of pollution:

> Um es ausführlicher zu erklären, könnte zum Beispiel ein jeder
> Picknickausflügler seinen eigenen Abfall mit nach Hause nehmen.

At first sight it seems you are in the middle of telling the reader what the individual can do to control pollution. If you look at it more precisely, you will see that it means that every picknicker can take his rubbish home to explain it – something – in greater detail. (You may be able to avoid this kind of nonsensical error by trying to reverse the sentence and see whether it still makes sense.)

Sometimes you can be too clever and by attempting to use what you think are sophisticated sentences, you can annoy the reader because you half-conceal quite a simple idea. An example for this would be:

> Nimmt man die Tatsachen in Kauf, so ist es möglich, festzustellen, daß
> viele Leute Sport als Zeitvertreib genießen.

If you mean to say that sport is a popular pastime, it is best to express this plainly and briefly, and save words to expand your ideas.

Avoid the commonplace

There are a number of levels at which this advice can be taken, and the level you take depends upon the degree of sophistication you wish to achieve. At the lowest level, it is a question of avoiding the sort of clichés we were talking about earlier, whilst at the highest level it is a question of adjusting the type of language you are using to make it match your subject matter in a way that is really creative or even artistic.

There is one type of expression found too often in essays which gives the impression that the writer has been too lazy to think about what is being written, and is content to be vague. This may not be the case, but if that is the impression the reader gets, then the effect is exactly the same as if it were true. Look at this sentence:

> Will man durch Deutschland fahren, so ist dieses mit dem Wagen, mit der Bahn, mit dem Fahrrad usw. möglich.

The inclusion of *usw.* here is unwise. What is really wrong with it?

Firstly, it is an abbreviation, and is not appropriate in the context of an essay. Since by definition an essay is a formal context, you should avoid using materials which may be acceptable in conversation, in lists (as *usw.*) or in informal letters or written directions.

Secondly, it is a colloquial expression. You should be careful about including colloquialisms or slang in an essay. You would not expect to read in a book on literature that 'this old chap wanted to live it up a bit, so fixed things up with the devil'. You might recognise it as the beginning of the plot of Goethe's 'Faust', but you would not accept the style comfortably. If you would not write like this in a serious English context, you must accept that the same is true for writing in German, and you must become aware of the social implications of the language you learn, as well as the literal meaning. To return to the German sentence above: it is not adequate either to write *usw.* in full. The whole expression is not suitable for an essay and should be replaced with some other expression. You could replace the list of means of transport by *so ist dieses mit verschiedenen Transportmitteln möglich*, with the added advantage that you have used less words than the original and so have more to use on less banal ideas.

Exercise 1

Find ways of avoiding using the expressions printed in italics. For example, 'In unserem Zeitalter sind Latein und Griechisch *nichts wert*' could become 'In unserem Zeitalter haben Latein und Griechisch keine große Bedeutung mehr.'

a. Ob man mit dem Zug fährt, *ist mir egal.*
b. Man *hat* über den Verlust von Fischen und Pflanzen *viel Krach gemacht.*
c. Das war eine Lösung, die *schiefgegangen ist.*
d. Das ist *dasselbe* für junge Leute.
e. Ich bin derselben Meinung wie die Leute, *die so denken.*
f. Die Arbeiter *hatten es satt*, für nichts zu arbeiten.
g. *Es macht nichts aus*, daß die Regierung anders denkt.
h. Auf dem Arbeitsamt ist Rat zu *kriegen.*
i. Es gibt *eine Menge* Gründe dafür, das zu rechtfertigen.
j. Dadurch, daß Chemikalien *und so was* in den Fluß fließt, wird natürlich eine wesentliche Wasserverschmutzung verursacht.

It is also advisable, if you want to make a better impression, to avoid common verbs such as *sein, machen, haben*; adjectives or adverbs like *schön, wichtig, schon*. It is not that they are not perfectly respectable parts of the German language, but you should where possible look for words that are more colourful, more active and less everyday. You might try to experiment by using the passive voice instead of the active; for example instead of 'Touristen besuchen oft diese Gegend', choose 'Diese Gegend wird oft von Touristen besucht'.

Exercise 2
Rewrite these sentences, finding other expressions to replace those printed in italics:

a. Dieser Mann *hat* einen guten Ruf.
b. In den Ballungsgebieten *sind* viele neue Siedlungen.
c. In der Rede, die er *machte, sprach* der Minister von Jugendproblemen.
d. Ein Kritiker sagte, daß er den Film nicht *gern hatte*.
e. Das Fernsehen ist in unserem Leben *wichtig* geworden.
f. Das Brandenburger Tor *ist* in der Mitte der Stadt und *ist* die Grenze zwischen West- und Ostberlin.
g. Man *macht* viel Wein in der Pfalz.
h. Die *Altstadt* hat viele *schöne* Gebäude.
i. Es *gibt* große Unterschiede zwischen den Parteien.
j. Solche modernen Apparate *machen* viel Vergnügen.

Exercise 3
Rewrite the following sentences, avoiding the expressions in italics:

a. *Ich glaube*, daß wir in Zukunft, wie schon in den meisten Ländern üblich, rechts fahren werden müssen.
b. *Es ist möglich*, daß wir zu viele Hausaufgaben bekommen.
c. *Ich hoffe*, daß dieses Problem zu beseitigen ist.
d. *Meiner Meinung nach* sollte man mit sechzehn Jahren Alkohol kaufen dürfen.
e. *Man glaubt*, daß der saure Regen Bäumen sehr schadet.
f. *Man hofft*, daß junge Leute besser ausgebildet werden können.
g. *Viele Leute glauben*, die staatliche Studienhilfe reicht längst nicht aus.
h. *Vielleicht* sollten Autofahrer regelmäßig geprüft werden.

Linking paragraphs

You also need to give careful thought to the way you link your paragraphs to each other. There are a number of ways of doing this, but there is one method we would recommend you to try which goes beyond linking them together by using a simple word or phrase.

Try and think of your essay as consisting of a single paragraph, consisting of as many sentences as there are main points in your essay. Then write this paragraph, with each sentence summing up the point to be made by the paragraph it represents. You will end up with a paragraph like this one, which deals with the topic 'Die Wirkung der Technik auf das moderne Leben':

> Man kann nicht leugnen, daß sich das Alltagsleben in unserem Jahrhundert durch außerordentliche technische Fortschritte verändert hat. Es ist jedoch frag lich, ob dieser Einfluß auch immer vorteilhaft gewesen ist. Es ist offensichtlich, daß wir heutzutage bequemer und gesunder leben, da unser Leben nicht so begrenzt ist. Dagegen hat man vielleicht zu viel von der 'guten alten Zeit' verloren: die ganze Hektik, die Angst vor der Zukunft, scheinbar unlösbare Weltprobleme erben wir von der Technik. Wir müssen uns also entscheiden, ob wir diese Technik zu günstigen Zwecken ausnützen und ob wir sie überhaupt beherrschen können.

Having done this, we can use each of these sentences to introduce each paragraph of the actual essay. In this way, the reader can actually follow the drift of your argument by glancing at the initial sentence of each paragraph, and, since you have previously written it as a coherent whole, your entire argument will of necessity appear much more coherent to your reader.

Look at the paragraph again. In writing these individual sentences in such a way that they go together to make up a coherent paragraph, we have linked them together naturally. Each is capable of expansion with example or explanation. The second sentence links with the first by posing a question about the undeniable statement on technology. The following sentence lends itself to examples of the benefits of technology, and the fourth to the drawbacks. The final sentence proposes the choice between chaos or control.

Looking at the structure of the sentences, they are also linked by various expressions of what people think or ask: *man kann nicht leugnen, es läßt sich jedoch fragen, es ist offensichtlich, hat man vielleicht, wir müssen uns also entscheiden.* However, no expression has been repeated. Writing your essay using this one-paragraph strategy is a good way to avoid repetition. Another important point illustrated by this paragraph is the usefulness of words like *jedoch, also, überhaupt,* which add emphasis to the points we are trying to make convincingly.

Exercise 4
Using the technique outlined above, write one paragraph on each of the essay titles given, in such a way that your paragraph could serve as a plan for a full essay:

a. Sollten Autofahrer frei sein, Alkohol zu trinken?
b. Ko-edukative Schulen: was halten Sie davon?

c.   'Studenten sollten sich auf das Studium konzentrieren, statt in den Ferien Arbeit zu suchen' Sind Sie auch dieser Meinung?

Some useful expressions

Here is a list of expressions you might find useful in various contexts. It is not intended to be exhaustive, but serves merely to give you a start in building up your own list. We recommend that you check in a good dictionary any expression (including those given below) of which you are not perfectly certain of the significance. Remember, too, the particular German flavour of additional words, referred to previously, such as *doch, noch, ja, schon, bestimmt, hauptsächlich, zwar, nämlich, bloß,* and the like.

Adding ideas

auch	noch	ferner	weiter
hinzu(fügen)	obendrein	außerdem	gleichfalls

Contrasting ideas

im Gegenteil	im Gegensatz (zu)	auf jeden Fall dagegen
jedoch	keineswegs	unterschiedlich

Making comparisons

einerseits/andererseits	ähnlich	gleich
im Vergleich zu	unter gleichen Umständen	

Making references

hinsichtlich	betreffend	wie schon bekannt
bezüglich	beispielsweise	was ... betrifft
zum Beispiel	es handelt sich um ...	

Expressing opinions

meiner Meinung/Ansicht nach		überzeugt
laut/nach	scheinen	sich vorstellen
wahrscheinlich	meines Erachtens	vermuten

Giving explanations

etwas in Kauf nehmen	offenbar	zweifellos	wirklich
grundsätzlich	tatsächlich	in der Tat	

Expressing consequences

infolgedessen	also	wirken auf	verursachen
das Ergebnis	sich ergeben		im wesentlichen

Analysing

im Grunde genommen	in erster Linie	überwiegend
an erster Stelle	überhaupt	

Chapter 7

Particular types of essay 1: Descriptive and narrative

These are two of the most difficult types of essay to write, because to write them competently requires much more literary skill than other types of essay, if you are to be really effective. Preparatory work in the form of careful reading (always with pencil in hand) is absolutely essential if you wish to reach a standard which will impress the reader as much as the types of essay we have looked at so far.

Descriptive essays

This is particularly true in the case of description. Whereas in the 'discussion' type of essay you may quite easily find yourself having too few words to play with in order to present your case effectively, when you are describing someone or something you may easily find it difficult to use the number of words you are required to use. In order to prove the point, try writing a description in English, 300 words long, of someone you know very well.

Choosing the order in which to present the information you want to give also constitutes a problem, and here again it is advisable to look carefully at the way skilled writers go about it. You will discover that there are a number of different ways, and you will have to choose whichever you feel you can manage best.

Let us take the case of describing the house in which you live. Obviously it would be possible to write a description which was purely factual, and limited to lists and sizes of rooms, and so forth. While this would give the reader some idea of what the house was like, it would, however, be unlikely to inspire great interest. You could embroider it a little, and make it look more like an estate agent's description, but here again it might not be very interesting, since most estate agents' descriptions do not give an all-round picture.

Presumably you wish to convey to the reader something of the character of the house, some of the atmosphere, which will conjure up also some ideas of the people who live in it, for there are always tell-tale signs in any house which tell you something about the inhabitants. There are two basic approaches possible: you can tell the reader about the house from your own point of view, picking out the things you feel are particularly significant, or you can look at it from the point of view of someone visiting the house for the first time, and describe what the visitor sees and what impression is gained.

If you consider the second method, you need to take the description step by step. Imagine the reader is in the street, then finds the house. How does it differ from the others either side or opposite? The reader turns towards the house, approaches the front door, perhaps through a garden, enters and passes from room to room. Of course if you live in a flat or in the country, your description will vary accordingly. You should beware of repetition – avoid *und dann . . ., dann.* Try to start each sentence differently. Sometimes these descriptions can be deceptively easy, but they usually test basic grammar as well as style and imagination.

Exercise 1
Write the following descriptions:

1. Your own home.
2. Making a cup of tea or coffee.
3. Your route to school or college.

When it comes to describing people, the same sort of approach can be adopted. When you meet someone for the first time, what do you notice? Is it his or her clothes, face, figure? It probably depends on the person, and you will have to decide which is more appropriate in each particular case. But in all cases, try and convey something of the personality of the person you are describing as suggested by outward appearances before going on to say something more specifically about the character. Above all, it is important to try and make your description interesting.

Exercise 2
Now write a description of someone you know. If a whole group of students is doing this, it can be interesting and useful (and amusing) to hand the various descriptions round, and see how easy it is to identify the people described. Alternatively, the whole group can write a description of one person, and then the descriptions can be compared; it will be useful to see what different people regard as being significant.

Exercise 3

1. Beschreiben Sie eine Stadt, die Sie gut kennen und wo Sie gern arbeiten würden.
2. Beschreiben Sie eine Gegend in Österreich oder Deutschland, die Sie besucht haben.
3. Sie gewinnen 1000DM im Lotto. Was würden Sie damit machen?

4. Beschreiben Sie eine bekannte Personlichkeit, die Sie besonders bewundern.
5. Beschreiben Sie einen Charakter in einem Buch, der Ihnen besonders aufgefallen ist.
6. Bildnis eines bekannten Sportlers.

Narrative

Theoretically, this should be the easiest kind of essay for you to write in German, because it is the kind of essay you will have done in earlier examinations. But there is of course a world of difference between the simple narrative you wrote in earlier papers and the kind of story you need to write to get a very high mark at A Level. The problem is how to make the transition from one to the other.

The secret lies, as it nearly always does, in doing things gradually, and not expecting to run before you can walk. Let us take a very simple narrative:

> Es war ein Sonntagmorgen. Ich wartete schon eine halbe Stunde am Parkplatz. Stefan war immer noch nicht da. Stefan war mein bester Freund, aber er wohnte in einer anderen Stadt und sollte mich hier im Dorf treffen. Wir hatten vor, von hier aus eine längere Wanderung zu machen. Gegen 10 Uhr sollten wir losgehen. Ich horte einen Wagen hinter mir bremsen und drehte mich um. Ja, Stefan war endlich angekommen. Er saß aber nicht am Steuer, sondern daneben im Beisitz. Er stieg aus und ich konnte sehen, daß er Krücken unter den Armen hatte. Erstaunt fragte ich ihn, was los sei. Es war offenbar nichts mit der Wanderung. Und wer war diese Frau am Steuer?

As a short story, this is hardly more than an outline, and some ending is required. Even the best short stories can be reduced to very simple terms, and it should not be too difficult to improve on this not only by lengthening it and by making the language more sophisticated, but also by introducing more in the way of characterisation, by adding more drama than there is at present. We can add a context that would not be there in more elementary examinations. For example, we could start this story in the following way:

> Seit Jahren schon waren Stefan und ich fest befreundet. Als Schulkameraden hatte er mir immer bei den Matheaufgaben geholfen, und ich hatte seine englischen Aufsätze korrigiert. Wir waren beide in einem Sportverein, spielten sogar in derselben Mannschaft und hatten viel zusammen erlebt. Aber jetzt sahen wir uns selten. Ich war Journalist geworden und Stefan arbeitete woanders als Ingenieur. Ich freute mich sehr über seinen Anruf vor ein paar Tagen. 'Wir müssen uns endlich treffen. Kennst du Kleindorf? Wie wäre es, wenn wir dort in der Nähe wandern und spater ein Gläschen trinken würden?'

Here we introduce the reader to the relationship of the two men and prepare for their reunion and outing. We also invite the suspicion that all may not go as planned – otherwise there would not be a story to tell.

We can build up to their meeting. A delay here is not only appropriate as the writer waits for his friend, but can lead to a faster and more dramatic pace when Stefan arrives. We could describe some of their escapades as boys, or could give a more detailed description of Stefan. Here is a possible interlude between introduction and action:

> Das letzte Mal, als wir zusammen waren, ja, das war im Sommer vor zwei Jahren. Das Studium war vorbei und in den letzten Wochen, ehe wir unser tägliches Brot verdienen mußten, trampten wir durch Frankreich. Stefan warf mir ständig vor, ich sei nach den langen Studienjahren faul und untauglich für so etwas geworden. Er war ein strammer Kerl, kerngesund, und wenn kein Wagen hielt, konnte er kilometerweit laufen, ohne sich über seinen schweren Rucksack zu beschweren. Eigentlich hatte er ja recht. Diese Wanderung heute zum Beispiel. Ich freute mich schon sehr auf das kommende Gespräch und wollte gern wissen, wie es ihm in seinem Beruf ging. Würde er aber im Galopp über Wiesen und durch Wälder laufen, während ich atemlos hinter ihm her keuchte?

You might not want to personalise the narrative by using the first person. You might decide to write it from the point of view of an outsider, using the third person. You may choose to tackle the story from Stefan's angle, or even from the woman's.

Now try to finish the rest of the story. Try to make it as interesting and lively as possible without overdoing it. If you exaggerate, you will have the opposite effect to the one you are trying to achieve.

Exercises

1. Expand and complete the following story, making it more interesting and dramatic.

    > Rolf Schneider saß zu Hause und sah fern. Aber er konnte sich schlecht konzentrieren. Ob er seiner Frau das alles erklären konnte? Würde sie Verständnis dafür haben? Daran, daß kein Geld mehr für den üblichen Sommerurlaub übrig war, war er selbst schuld. Plötzlich klingelte es. Schneider stand auf und ging zur Tür. Wer könnte es wohl noch sein, so spät am Abend? Vor ihm stand ein Fremder. 'Herr Schneider? Ich gratuliere! Sie haben den großen Lotteriepreis gewonnen!'

2. Hier is a brief outline of a not very interesting story: write the story in not more than 300 words, making it as interesting and dramatic as possible:
    Anruf von einem Freund – Einladung zu einer Radtour – Vorbereitungen

– Ankunft am Treffpunkt – niemand da – nach Hause fahren – Freund anrufen – was weiter geschieht.

3. Here is another brief and uninteresting outline of a story: using no more than 300 words, write as lively a story as possible.: Weihnachten – Rückfahrt nach England mit der Fähre – Sturm – Schiff kann nicht anlegen – was passiert?

4. Sie haben einen Schiffbruch erlitten und sind nun auf einer einsamen, verlassenen Insel gestrandet. Erzählen Sie, wie Sie dieses Abenteuer überlebt haben.

5. Der schönste Tag meines Lebens.

Chapter 8

Particular types of essays 2: Argumentative

When you have reached this chapter you should not really need much more in the way of guidance where argumentative essays are concerned, because, with the exception of the chapter on descriptive and narrative essays, virtually all our models have been of that type. Consequently, if you still have any doubts about how to start tackling a subject, how to present your case, how to introduce it or how to draw it to a conclusion, you should refer back to the chapter concerned.

What we are going to do in this chapter is to take three topics, from the list given in Chapter 10, and show you *one* way of writing each essay, following the advice given in earlier chapters. We are not suggesting that the way these essays are written is the only way they could be written, nor that these are 'model answers' in the sense that they could not be bettered. On the contrary, we have deliberately tried to write them in such a way as to present you with an approachable target: it seems to us that there is little point in attempting to write like a sophisticated German speaker: we are therefore concentrating on showing you that it is possible to write good essays using the sort of German that should be within the grasp of A level candidates.

1. *Inwiefern sind wir als Einzelne für unsere Umwelt verantwortlich?*

   Das Konzept Umweltschutz ist bekannt aber nicht leicht zu erklären. Es hängt eng mit der Erkenntnis zusammen, daß wir alle: Menschen, Tiere und Pflanzen, voneinander abhängig sind. Eine Zerstörung dieser ökologischen Balance schädigt daher nicht nur unsere Umwelt sondern auch unsere Lebensqualität.

   Um gesund zu leben braucht der Mensch eine heile, gesunde Umwelt. Luftverpestung, Wasserbeschädigung, schädlicher Chemikaliengebrauch, um nur einige Beispiele zu nennen, tragen zur Mißhandlung unserer Umwelt dermaßen bei, daß wir quasi Selbstmord begehen.

   Der Beitrag des Einzelnen im Kampf um die Aufrechterhaltung unserer Umwelt ist vielleicht gering, aber trotzdem nicht weniger wichtig. Um umweltbewußt zu leben, sollte man sich im eigenen Haushalt umsehen und einmal aufzählen, wo Änderungen umweltfreundlicher sein könnten. Ist unser Wasserverbrauch zu hoch? Benutzen wir zu viele Chemikalien? Zu viel unnötiges Papier? (Unsere Wälder werden jedes Jahr geringer). Wie steht es mit unserem Auto oder Moped? Und benutzen wir zuviel Plastik?

Schon als Konsument könnte man dadurch einflußreicher sein, daß man verantwortungsvoller kauft. Firmen reagieren schnell, wenn ihre umweltfeindlichen Produkte nicht mehr verkauft werden können, und würden darum vielleicht alternative Herstellungs-materialien suchen.

Aber unser Beitrag zur Umwelterhaltung ist mit diesen Maßnahmen nicht beendet. Wir haben das demokratische Recht, uns gegen Dinge zu wehren, die unsere bürgerliche Sicherheit gefährden. Staat und Industrie könnten oft schnellere und effektive Maßnahmen zum Umweltschutz einführen, und auch darauf achten, daß sie beachtet werden. Wenn dies dann nicht geschieht, ist es unserem Verantwortungsgefühl überlassen sich zu wehren.

Bürgerinitiativen, politische Zusammenarbeit zum Wohl der Gemeinschaft ist eine bessere Lösung als extreme Maßnahmen, wie zum Beispiel Demonstrationen, aber trotzdem genau so ernst gemeint.

Unsere Lebensqualität in der Industriegesellschaft zu erhalten ist die Verantwortung des Einzelnen, genau wie man auch als Einzelner durch weitere Umweltzerstörung leiden würde.

2. *'Alte Menschen: die vergessene Minderheitsgruppe heutzutage.'*
Nehmen Sie dazu Stellung.

Die hergebrachte Annahme, daß alte Menschen in ihrem Alter von jüngeren Verwandten betreut werden, ist heute leider weitgehend ausgestorben. Dadurch, daß junge Ehepaare nach ihrer Heirat oft heutzutage nicht nur das Elternhaus verlassen. sondern auch aus der Umgebung ziehen, hat eine Änderung der Familienstruktur von der traditionellen Großfamilie zur Kernfamilie stattgefunden. Alte Menschen, wie die Eltern, sind sich dann oft in ihrem Lebensabend selbst überlassen, also zu einer Zeit, wo sie am meisten Hilfe benötigen.

Dazu kommt, daß unsere hektische, moderne Lebensweise es uns oft nicht erlaubt, sie regelmäßig zu besuchen, und so verliert man schnell Kontakt und findet es sogar manchmal belästigend, wenn unsere Hilfe in Anspruch genommen werden muß.

Das Leben in einem Altersheim scheint dann eine gute Alternative für ältere Menschen, besonders wenn sie pflegebedürftig sind. Dabei vergißt man leicht, daß sie Individualisten sind, die trotz

Gebrechlichkeit ihre geistigen Fakultäten zu erhalten suchen. Oft fühlen sie sich dann nicht nur abgelehnt, sondern auch verlassen und vergessen.

Der Staat ermutigt ältere Menschen auch wenig im Alter einen wertvollen Beitrag für die Gesellschaft zu Leisten. Mit 60–65 Jahren werden sie pensioniert und erhalten oft eine Rente, die den bisherigen Lebenstil nicht ermöglicht.

Dank moderner medizinischer Betreuung hat sich unser Lebensalter verlängert und man sollte in Betracht ziehen, daß ältere Menschen auf Grund ihrer Lebenserfahrungen viel beizutragen haben. Wir sollten daher alte Leute nutzen anstatt sie beiseite zu schieben. Dabei genügen Altersklubs, Konzessionen zu Abendklassen, Theaterbesuchen und dergleichen nicht, sondern man sollte weitere Möglichkeiten finden, diese Senioren auch jetzt noch ins moderne Leben einzuschließen, und sie als eine nützliche Gruppe unserer Gesellschaft anzuerkennen.

Eine Minderheitsgruppe mögen alte Menschen wohl sein, aber sollten sie darum vergessen werden? Oder tun wir das so bereitwillig, weil sie uns ermahnen, daß auch wir älter werden? Man sollte sich fragen, wie man seinen eigenen Lebensabend verbringen möchte, und sich dann für unsere Seniorengruppe mehr einsetzen, um ihren Lebensabend so wertvoll wie möglich zu gestalten.

3.   *Sollte jede Schule eine Raucherecke einrichten?*

Bis vor einigen Jahren gehörte der Tabakverbrauch so sehr zu unserem Lebensstil, daß sich kaum jemand Gedanken darüber machte, ob das Rauchen gesundheitsschädlich sei oder nicht. Aber jetzt ist es als eine besonders gesundheitsgefährdende Angewohnheit anerkannt, die sogar zur Nikotinabhängigkeit führen könnte. Warum dann sollten Schulen Raucherecken einrichten, anstatt eine derartig schädliche Angewohnheit zu unterdrücken?

Jugendliche rauchen oft, weil es für sie ein Statussymbol ist, ein Zeichen, daß sie zur Gruppe gehören und von dieser als gleichberechtigt anerkannt sind. Aufhören zu Rauchen würde nicht nur als Schwäche angesehen werden, sondern könnte auch zur Ausschließung von der Gruppe führen. Also wird weitergeraucht.

Wenn nun in der Schule das Rauchen kategorisch verboten wird, trifft man sich eben heimlich auf Toiletten, in Ecken oder Gängen, um es trotzdem zu tun. Das verleiht dann einen besonderen heimlichen Reiz, der wieder zu einer negativen Solidarität führt. Abgesehen davon ist es auch feuergefährlich, denn Kippen, schnell weggeworfen, wenn man entdeckt wird, brennen oft weiter und können viel Schaden anrichten.

Eine Raucherecke wäre auch ein bestimmter Ort, wo Raucher beisammen sind undes sich dadurch eine gute Gelegenheit bietet zu versuchen, sie von ihrer Angewohnheit abzubringen. Außerdem können Nichtraucher dann auch den ihnen gefährlichen Qualm vermeiden.

Es wäre unrealistisch anzunehmen, daß ein Schulrauchverbot das Rauchen unter Jugendlichen unterdrücken würde und auch darum ist die Einrichtung einer Raucherecke angebracht. Schüler brauchen sich nicht in Ecken herumdrücken, es gibt keinen Grund gegen ein solches Verbot zu rebellieren und man könnte sie vielleicht positiv beeinflussen, das Rauchen aufzugeben.

Eines muß jedoch noch bemerkt werden. Obwohl Jugendliche oft schon frühzeitig zu rauchen beginnen, wissen Eltern oft nichts von dieser Angewohnheit ihrer Kinder. Es sollte daher von der Schule eine Elternerlaubnis verlangt werden, sonst könnte sie leicht in Schwierigkeiten geraten. Denn es wird ja erwartet, daß Schulen mit gutem Beispiel vorangehen und für ihre Beschlüsse den Eltern gegenüber verantwortlich sind.

Chapter 9

Particular types of essay 3: Letters and dialogues

Letters

It would be tempting to think that when you are asked to write a letter in an examination, at least then you might be less restricted by the form, because when you write a letter in real life, you tend to sit down and start writing without regard to construction, development of argument, or any of the other things we have talked about so far. But you would be wrong, because you must remember that you are still writing an essay that has to be assessed, and therefore your aim must still be to impress. Of course you can write a chatty letter in interesting and correct German and earn yourself a good mark; but it is only right that if that interesting letter were constructed in a more careful way it would get a higher mark. What is more, even if you are writing to a friend and not for an examiner, it is surely a mark of the regard in which you hold your friend if you have clearly taken the trouble to think about how you present what you are writing, especially if the subject of your letter is a serious one; in an examination, of course, the subject matter will nearly always be serious.

Beginning and ending letters
You should remember from your O Level/GCSE days that there are a number of different ways of opening and closing a letter, according to whether your letter is a formal or an informal one, depending on the nature of your relationship with your correspondent. We do not therefore intend to waste space here going over all the possibilities, because there are more important aspects to consider; let us simply remind you that you need to provide your letter with a beginning and an ending that are appropriate.

Placing the subject matter in context
But you do need to remember that what you are writing is supposed to be a letter, even if the subject matter is such that it seems more like an essay in disguise. Consequently, immediately after greeting the person to whom you are writing, you need to place your subject in context. Perhaps the best way to illustrate this is to take an actual question as an example:

Ein junger Deutscher, der Anglistik studiert, erklärt in einem Brief an einen Freund/an eine Freundin, warum er für ein einjähriges Studium im Ausland die Vereinigten Staaten gewählt hat.

There might be two circumstances in which you would write such a letter:

a. your friend does not know you have left Germany to spend time abroad, and you are writing to tell him/her the news;
b. your friend does know you are in the United States, presumably from a previous letter, and wonders why you have chosen the United States instead of Britain or any other English-speaking country.

So your opening paragraph could be either:

Boston, den 20. Oktober

Lieber Karl!

    Du wirst Dich sicher wundern, daβ Du einen Brief von mir aus Boston bekommst, und nicht aus München. Ich bin schon seit zwei Wochen hier, natürlich um Englisch zu studieren. Du wirst wohl fragen, warum ich in Amerika bin, und der 'reinen' Sprache der Engländer den Rücken gekehrt habe. Ich möchte Dir also die Gründe genau erklären.

or

Lieber Karl!

    Es war überhaupt keine Überraschung, Deinen Brief zu bekommen, in dem Du mich fragst, warum bloβ Amerika. Da ich unglaublich wenig Zeit vor meiner Abfahrt hatte, ist dies die erste Gelegenheit, Dir alles genau erklären zu können.

The heart of the matter
Obviously, the more realistic you make your explanation the more impressive your essay is likely to be, and this means that you must have thought out valid reasons for your choice. It will be a personal interpretation but should be expressed in an orderly and logical fashion. Assuming you discard personal reasons, like having relations in America, or a boy/girl friend here, work out the arguments and write a paragraph on each. The main part of your letter might then look like this:

Erstens wollte ich ein nichteuropaisches Land besuchen. Ich kenne Groβbritannien gewissermaβen, wenn man ein anderes Land gut kennen kann, und werde sicher noch mehrmals hinfahren. Amerika ist ein anderer Kontinent, mit seinen eigenen Landschaften, Lebensweisen und Problemen. Da wir Europäer Amerika praktisch nur durch die Medien kennen, vor allem durch Filme und Fernsehen, wollte ich persönlich erleben, wie es nun wirklich ist. Und da ich ein ganzes Jahr zur Verfügung hatte, schien es gerade richtig, als Student mit anderen Studenten zu leben, die aus allen Ecken der USA stammen.

Als zweiter Grund wollte ich sowieso Naheres über das Land erfahren, das so zweifelslos eine bedeutende und einflußreiche Weltmacht ist. Die Vereinigten Staaten haben eine sehr bedeutende Rolle in der heutigen Weltpolitik zu erfüllen: sie sollen ein Gleichgewicht zwischen Krieg und Frieden aufrecht erhalten. Doch als vielleicht das reichste Land der Welt, ist diese Republik nicht ohne Probleme – Armut, Drogensucht herrschen auch hierzulande. Obwohl meine Erfahrungen unvermeidlich begrenzt bleiben, will ich trotzdem soviel wie möglich sehen und erleben und habe deshalb vor, in den Semesterferien woanders hin zu fahren. Vielleicht habe ich bis dann auch ein paar Amerikaner näher kennengelernt.

Die vielseitige Kultur zog mich auch an, und zwar nicht nur die von Europa beeinflußte, wie etwa Literatur. In einem Land, wo Englisch die Hauptsprache ist, gibt es trotzdem so sehr viele Einflusse aus anderen Kulturen, wie der spanischen, oder der einheimischen Indianerkultur, um nur zwei Beispiele zu nennen.

Rounding it off

You need to round off your letter in a natural way, for the same reason as you needed to open it naturally. But there is as little justification for repetition and summarising in a letter as there is in any other essay, and, at least for examination purposes, you need to keep fairly closely to the topic on which you are asked to write. Even so, there are many possibilities, such as the one we offer:

Es war also einerseits nicht schwer, mich für Amerika zu entscheiden, obgleich ich doch etwas gezögert habe. Ein ganzes Jahr in einer vollig fremden Welt zu verbringen, fern von zu Hause, von Familie und Bekanntschaft, aber trotzdem eine Möglichkeit, etwas Neues zu lernen! Aber meine Erlebnisse bis jetzt haben meine Wahl schon gerechtfertigt, obwohl ich erst seit zwei Wochen hier bin. Aber darüber mehr in meinem nächsten Brief!

Bis dann, herzliche Grüße,
Ulrich.

Dialogues

We made a reference earlier to carrying on a dialogue, but what we were describing was a sort of internal dialogue, where you are yourself putting forward an argument and then countering it with another one. But this is not what the Examination Boards have in mind when they actually ask you to write a dialogue, because in that case you have to make it appear as if two people were involved, not just yourself; generally this will involve either pretending to be having a discussion with someone or pretending to interview someone, and it is important to realise that the difference between the demands these two tasks make is considerable. If you are having a discussion, the implication is that both characters involved put forward their own point of view, each probably contradicting the other. If it is an interview, one person is asking questions, and the other one is providing answers to those questions.

Characterisation

Whichever type is involved, however, you need to remember that spoken language is different from written language, and that, although you will obviously be writing down what is said, it is supposed to look as if it really might have been said by someone. This does not necessarily mean that you have to use slang or sloppy language, but it does mean that, in order to be really impressive you need to be alive to the sort of expressions which are really too literary to be used in speech, except speech of the most formal kind.

It means, too, that you have to 'get inside the skin' of your characters to a certain extent, because unless you differentiate between the characters involved in your dialogue, the argument you are presenting will appear confusing and dull. You need, then, to decide beforehand what attitudes will be displayed by each character, and what aspects of their personality will be revealed by what they say.

Presenting the argument

1. Conversations

Characterisation apart, however, the approach is basically the same as that described earlier, in relation to the essay topic:

Was halten Sie vom Rauchen?

in that we were presenting two conflicting points of view, and if you wrote it as a dialogue between two people you would be able to use exactly the same points as were made before. Only the presentation would be different as, not only would the style have to vary, but the introduction and conclusion would have to be altered to fit into the context of a discussion which needs a beginning and an end.

2. Interviews

We also referred earlier to the raising of a number of questions which your essay would need to answer, and this is essentially what the interview calls for. It is different from the conversation described above in one important respect: whereas in a conversation it is the point of view of both participants which matters, in an interview you are trying to find out the point of view of one person only. Obviously, the choice of questions matters a great deal, but the best interviews tend to be those where the interviewer says very little and the person being interviewed says a lot, being stimulated by cleverly posed questions.

The effective interview you see on television or hear on radio, however, is by no means always spontaneous, and the printed interview will have been edited. Very often the interviewee will have decided beforehand what he or she wants to say and the questions are made up in such a way as to allow him or her to say it; there is no reason why you should not do the same when writing this type of essay. Some interviews you see, however, give the impression that, whereas the speaker has already decided what to say, the questions have not been framed accordingly; the result is that he or she appears to be avoiding answering the question. On television and radio, politicians especially appear to get away with this, but there is no need for you to try, because you are providing both the questions and the answers. Make sure they fit together!

An example
Interview mit einer älteren Berlinerin. Sie sind der Reporter. (250 Words)

Interviewer: Berlin hat sich bestimmt sehr in Ihrer Lebenszeit verändert, nicht wahr?

Berlinerin: Ja, das schon. Berlin war eine Weltstadt, und hier war immer viel los. Aber während des Krieges wurden wir mehrmals ausgebombt, und wir lebten in Trümmern und verhungerten fast.

Interviewer: Und trotzdem sind Sie hier geblieben?

Berlinerin: Ja. Ich heiratete nach dem Krieg, und wir erhielten eine neue Wohnung. Außerdem waren meine Verwandten auch noch hier. – Aber jetzt wohnen viele im Osten, und seitdem die Mauer errichtet wurde, konnten wir uns jahrelang nicht sehen. Nur über die Mauer winken konnte man. Aber jetzt ist es ein bißchen besser.

Interviewer: Und was bietet Berlin heute?

Berlinerin: Sehr viel. Es gibt die berühmte Philharmonie, viele Theater und zahlreiche Kunstgalerien. Außerdem liegt um Berlin eine herrliche Seenlandschaft mit vielen Wäldern.

Interviewer: Und die Nachteile?

Berlinerin: Wir sind Insulaner, von der DDR umgeben, das spürt man. Überall sind Grenzen.

Interviewer: Gibt es auch Sozialprobleme?

Berlinerin: Ja, erstens hat Berlin zu viele alte Leute. Dann gefallen mir die Drogensüchtigen und Ausgeflippten nicht, die oft am Bahnhof Zoo herumlungern. Im Kreuzberg wohnen viele Gastarbeiterfamilien, die oft sprachliche und kulturelle Schwierigkeiten haben, sich unserem Lebensstil anzupassen. Das braucht Zeit.

Interviewer: Was würden Sie einem Berlin-Besucher empfehlen?
Berlinerin: Abgesehen von den vielen Museen, vielleicht zuerst den
               Kurfürstendamm mit seinen vielen eleganten Geschäften,
               Cafés und Restaurants. Dann auch den Breitscheidplatz mit
               dem schönen Europa-Center, wo es immer etwas interes-
               santes zu sehen und zu tun gibt. Und abends zum Theater
               oder Cabaret und danach in eine Kneipe. Berlin schläft nie.
Interviewer: Ja ich merke: Berlin ist eine Reise wert. Ich danke Ihnen.

Exercises

1.   Sie schreiben an die Redaktion einer Zeitung über die Pläne eines
     neuen Einkaufszentrums, die Ihnen nicht gefallen. (300 words)

2.   Mutter und Vater entscheiden, wieviel Taschengeld sie ihrem sieb-
     zehnjährigen Kind geben wollen (350 words)

3.   Sie vergleichen mit einem deutschen/österreichischen Freund die
     Unterschiede im Bildungswesen in den beiden Ländern. (350 words).

4.   Diskussionsthema: Ein Freund/eine Freundin hält sehr viel vom Jagen,
     aber Sie haben Tiere sehr gern. (300 words)

5.   Ein Interview mit einem bekannten Sportler. (300 words)

Chapter 10

Practice essay topics

Politics and the modern world
1. Großbritannien und die Europäische Gemeinschaft.
2. Warum existiert Ausländerfeindlichkeit in unserem Land und wie könnte man sie bekämpfen?
3. Die Schweiz hat einen Präsidenten und England eine Königin. Welches Staatssystem würden Sie vorziehen? Warum?
4. Probleme der sogenannten Dritten Welt.
5. 'Die Gleichheit der Gelegenheit ist eine von Politikern erfundene Fabel' – Was halten Sie davon?
6. In Ihrer Gegend ist eine Kernanlage geplant. Würden Sie diesem Plan zustimmen? Was ist Ihre Stellung dazu?
7. Europas Verpflichtung der 'Dritten' Welt gegenüber.
8. Welcher Politiker hat Ihrer Ansicht nach den größten Einfluß auf die Politik Europas im 20. Jahrhundert ausgeübt?
9. Die Bedeutung der Arabischen Staaten heute.
10. Wie könnte man den Hunger der Welt bekämpfen?
11. Inwiefern sind wir als Einzelne für unsere Umwelt verantwortlich?
12. 'Unsere Landschaft ist im Begriff, ein Müllhaufen zu werden'. Was meinen Sie dazu?
13. Beeinflussen Demonstrationen wirklich politische Entscheidungen?
14. Kann der Einzelne das heutige politische Geschehen beeinflussen?
15. Leben wir tatsächlich im 'Zeitalter der Angst'?

Germany, Austria and Switzerland
1. Wie stellen Sie sich die Schweiz vor? Würden Sie gern dort leben? Warum?
2. Deutschland – eine Nation?
3. Was wissen Sie von den wichtigsten Familienfeiern in einem dieser Länder?
4. Kann man tatsächlich einen guten Eindruck von einem Land erhalten, wenn man nur etwas darüber liest?
5. Wie wichtig ist der Wintersport in Österreich oder in der Schweiz?

6. Geben Sie das Interview wieder zwischen Ihnen als Reporter und dem Bürgermeister eines kleinen Ortes.
7. Außern Sie sich zum Gastarbeiterproblem in der Bundesrepublik.
8. Es wird oft behauptet, daβ die deutsche Wohlstandsgesellschaft den Einzelnen vergiβt. Meinen Sie, daβ das nur ein deutsches Problem ist?
9. Was ist die Attraktion Österreichs? Warum fahren so viele Touristen jährlich dorthin?
10. Kann ein Staat auch heutzutage noch seine Neutralität aufrechthalten?
11. Wie wichtig sind die deutschen Wälder?
12. Warum verlassen so viele Jugendliche jährlich ihr Elternhaus, um in Städten zu arbeiten? Beziehen Sie sich in Ihrer Antwort entweder auf die Schweiz oder auf Österreich.

The social scene
1. Vor- und Nachteile der Ehe oder des freien Zusammenlebens.
2. Wie könnte das Arbeitslosenproblem vielleicht gelöst werden?
3. Das Asylanten-Problem Deutschlands.
4. Wie könnte die Lebensqualität unserer modernen Gesellschaft verbessert werden?
5. Denken Sie, es ist gut in der heutigen Zeit zu leben?
6. Altwerden – ein Problem? Was denken Sie darüber?
7. 'Ehepaare wollen oft nur zwei Kinder'. Was halten Sie davon?
8. 'Alte Menschen: die vergessene Minderheitsgruppe heutzutage'. Nehmen Sie dazu Stellung.
9. 'Die Geldsucht ist der Fluch unserer Gesellschaft'.
10. 'Man sollte nicht jugendliche Straftäter, sondern deren Eltern bestrafen.' Ist diese Behauptung richtig?
11. Untersuchen Sie die möglichen Ursachen der heutigen Arbeitslosigkeit. Wie sehen Sie die Zukunft?
12. 'Kleider machen Leute'. Inwiefern gilt dieses Sprichwort für junge Leute?
13. Kann man sich tatsächlich in einer modernen Groβstadt wohlfühlen?
14. Bürgerinitiativen: was denken Sie darüber?
15. Erklären Sie, warum Sie vielleicht Sozialarbeiter(in) werden mochten.

Youth
1. Ist es schwerer, heute jung zu sein als vor dreiβig Jahren?
2. 'Junge Menschen heute sind verantwortungslos!' Stimmt das wirklich?
3. Denken Sie, daβ sich Ihre Generation sehr von der Ihrer Eltern unterscheidet?
4. Was sind Ihrer Meinung nach die 'wichtigen Dinge' im Leben?
5. Jung und alt; wie könnte man den Generationskonflikt überbrücken?
6. 'Zuviel Geld und zuviel Freiheit'. Ist diese Behauptung richtig?
7. Das Drogenproblem unserer Zeit.
8. Sollte jede Schule eine Raucherecke einrichten?

9. Warum Popmusik?
10. Untersuchen Sie das Problem der Jugendarbeitslosigkeit.
11. Man spricht von einer 'Disko-Kultur'. Was verstehen Sie unter diesem Begriff?
12. Mit welchen Problemen beschäftigen sich junge Menschen heute?

Women

1. 'Die Frau ist nicht frei, weil sie keine Freizeit hat.' Was denken Sie?
2. Die Gleichberechtigung der Frau – Tatsache oder Erfindung?
3. Die Rolle der Frau in der Politik des 20. Jahrhunderts.
4. Warum stehen auch heute noch so wenig Frauen im öffentlichen Leben?
5. Können Frauen gleichzeitig berufstätig und Mütter sein?

General philosophical

1. 'Ab heute pflücke die Rosen des Lebens'. Was halten Sie von Ronsards Rat?
2. Der Wert der Tradition.
3. Welche Grenzen sollte man der Toleranz setzen?
4. 'Reisen erzieht' und 'Jede Trennung ist ein kleines Sterben'. Meinen Sie, diese beiden Sprichwörter widersprechen sich?
5. Welche Überlegungen würden vielleicht Ihre Wahl eines Lebenspartners beeinflussen?
6. 'Arbeit ist ein notwendiges Übel'. Stimmt das?
7. Stimmen Sie mit dem Motto 'Zurück zur Natur' überein?
8. 'Es ist ein böser Wind, der nichts gutes bringt'. Können Sie dieses Sprichwort durch eine Anekdote illustrieren?
9. Sehnen Sie sich zur 'guten, alten Zeit' zurück?
10. Denken Sie, daß Hobbys Zeitverschwendung sind?
11. Untersuchen Sie, warum Menschen ihre Heimat verlassen.
12. Ist es noch zeitgemäß, Festtage zu feiern?
13. 'Der Mensch baut zu viele Mauern und zu wenige Brücken', (I. Newton). Wie trifft das auch auf unsere Zeit zu?
14. Kann man tatsächlich ohne Vorurteile durchs Leben gehen?
15. Unsere Welt hat sich verkleinert – aber hat sie sich auch verbessert?

Sport

1. Sollte man durch Sport auch Geld verdienen?
2. Sollten gefährliche Sportarten untersagt werden?
3. Wie beurteilen Sie die Behauptung, daß Sport eine Zeitverschwendung ist?
4. Man sagt, Sport ist gesund. Gibt es auch noch andere Vorteile?
5. Sport und Politik.
6. Warum wird heute wohl soviel Sport getrieben?
7. Es wird behauptet, daß Sport die Völker zusammenbringt. Was meinen Sie?
8. Was halten Sie vom Leistungssport?

Education

1. Können Lehrer durch Computer ersetzt werden?
2. Was haben Sie durch Ihre Schulausbildung in der Oberstufe erzielt?
3. Denken Sie, daß die Schule auf das Leben vorbereitet?
4. 'Die Schulzeit ist die schönste Zeit'. Stimmen Sie mit dieser Ansicht überein?
5. Prüfungen – das notwendige Übel.
6. Beurteilen Sie das deutsche Schulsystem.
7. Sollten die Privatschulen in Ihrem Land abgeschafft werden?
8. 'Es ist des Lernens kein Ende'. Stimmen Sie mit diesem Spruch überein?
9. Sind Schüler tatsächlich nur 'Konsumenten'?
10. Inwiefern sollte das Fernsehen auch im Unterricht eine Rolle spielen?
11. 'In unserem Zeitalter der Technik sollte der Unterricht sich auch dementsprechend anpassen.' Was meinen Sie?
12. Das Problem des Geldverdienens für Schüler.

Travel

1. Wohin würden Sie fahren, wenn Sie die Gelegenheit hätten, ein Jahr im Ausland zu verbringen, und was würden Sie dort tun?
2. Sie wollten einen Monat mit Ihrer Studentenfahrkarte durch Europa reisen. Welche Überlegungen würden Ihre Reiseroute bestimmen?
3. Warum wird auch heute noch so viel gewandert?
4. Wie lernt man ein fremdes Land am besten kennen?
5. Warum sind Jugendherbergen auch heute noch beliebt?
6. Beschreiben Sie Ihre erste Reise allein ins Ausland.

Description

1. Beschreiben Sie jemand, dem Sie gern ähneln möchten und erklären Sie warum.
2. Eine unvergeßliche Person.
3. Das Portrait eines alten Mannes/einer alten Frau.
4. Beschreiben Sie, wie der Ort, in dem Sie leben, sich in den letzten 10 Jahren verändert hat. Hat er sich verbessert oder verschlechtert?
5. Mein erster Kontakt mit einem Auslander.
6. Unser Hund – unser Freund.
7. Der Schulaustausch.

Imaginative narration

1. Ein Alptraum.
2. Auf dem Weg nach Osterreich haben Sie einen Unfall gesehen. Beschreiben Sie die Szene.
3. Ihr Flugzeug mußte eine Notlandung in den Bergen machen. Beschreiben Sie wie das geschah, und wie Sie gerettet wurden.
4. Sie sind der Sohn/die Tochter eines berühmten Fabrikanten und wurden gekidnappt. Beschreiben Sie, was dann geschah.
5. Eine gefährliche Mission.

6. Man hat einige jahrhundertalte Bäume abgesägt, um für eine neue Autobahn Platz zu machen. Was halten Sie davon?
7. Eines Morgens wachen Sie auf, ohne sich zu erinnern, wer Sie sind. Erzählen Sie weiter.
8. Wie stellen Sie sich das Leben im 21. Jahrhundert vor?
9. Nach einem Schiffbruch befinden Sie sich auf einer verlassenen Insel. Beschreiben Sie die ersten Stunden dort.
10. Meine erste Fahrstunde.

Literature and the arts
1. Was sind die wesentlichen Eigenschaften eines guten Romans?
2. Sie schreiben Kriminalromane. Wie beginnt Ihr nächster Roman?
3. Wie können Bücher und Zeitschriften Ihre Meinung über Ausländer beeinflussen?
4. Sollte der Staat die bildenden Künste unterstützen?
5. Warum sind Taschenbücher so beliebt?
6. Der deutsche Beitrag zur Kunst im 20. Jahrhundert.
7. Ein Nachmittag, den Sie in einem Museum verbrachten.
8. Die Rolle des Künstlers in unserer Gesellschaft.
9. Sind Museen wirklich langweilig?
10. Eine Bibliothek auf Rädern – was halten Sie von dieser Idee?

Cinema, television and radio
1. Hat das Kino auch heute noch eine Rolle zu erfüllen?
2. Was für Qualitäten sollte ein guter Intendant besitzen?
3. Stimmt es, daß das Kino in den letzten 20 Jahren seine Popularität eingebüßt hat?
4. Inwieweit trägt die Musik zum Erfolg eines Filmes bei?
5. Der Einfluß des Fernsehens auf junge Menschen.
6. Stimmen Sie mit der Ansicht überein, daß es mehr Gewalttätigkeit im Fernsehen gibt, als gut ist?
7. Die Bedeutung des Lokalradios.
8. Vor- und Nachteile des Fernsehens.
9. Inwiefern wird das Familienleben von den sogenannten Massenmedien beeinflußt?
10. Kann die Verfilmung eines Buches das Lesen wirklich ersetzen?

Advertising
1. Sollte viel Geld für Werbung ausgegeben werden?
2. Wird unsere Gesellschaft positiv oder negativ durch die Werbung beeinflußt?
3. Was halten Sie vom alljährlichen 'Weihnachtsrummel'?
4. Welchen Einfluß auf unser alltägliches Leben hat die Fernseh-Werbung?

Industry and technology
1. Vor- und Nachteile der Kernkraftanlagen.
2. Was ist Ihrer Meinung nach die einflußreichste Erfindung unseres Jahrhunderts? Rechtfertigen Sie Ihren Standpunkt.
3. Ist das Auto ein Problem heutzutage – oder?
4. 'Die Technik soll dem Menschen dienen, ihn aber nicht beherrschen.' Was halten Sie davon?
5. Industrie, Technologie und Natur: läßt sich das vereinbaren?

Work
1. Das Verhältnis der Arbeit und Freizeit in unserem Leben.
2. Welchen Beruf finden Sie beneidenswert?
3. Zwei junge Menschen diskutieren: Der Eine möchte studieren, der Andere möchte sofort nach Schulabschluß anfangen zu arbeiten. Wie wird diese Unterhaltung wohl verlaufen? Wer trifft die richtige Entscheidung?
4. Denken Sie, Ärzte und Krankenschwestern sollten das Streikrecht haben?
5. Warum könnte die Freizeit ein Problem sein?
6. Ihre Schule hat es Ihnen ermöglicht, einige Wochen in einem Betrieb zu arbeiten. Beschreiben Sie, was geschah.

The future
1. Wie stellen Sie sich das Leben in den kommenden 50 Jahren vor?
2. Sollten Roboter tatsächlich Menschen ersetzen?
3. 'Die Technik verändert das Gesicht der Erde' – Nehmen Sie dazu Stellung.
4. Wird unsere Zukunft schon in der Gegenwart bestimmt?
5. Wie wird die Technik des 20. Jahrhunderts auch in der Zukunft das Leben beinflussen?

War and peace
1. Sie wohnen in einem wehrpflichtigen Land. Welche Gründe würden Sie zur Wehrdienstverweigerung angeben?
2. 'Es ist in der Natur des Menschen, Krieg zu führen'.
3. Wie können wir als Einzelne zu einem Weltfrieden beitragen?

The Police
1. Warum brauchen wir die Polizei?
2. Sollte man Polizisten bewaffnen oder nicht?
3. Wie könnte das Verhältnis zwischen Polizei und Bürger verbessert werden?

Animals
1. Es gibt zu viele Haustiere in den Städten. Denken Sie das auch?

2. Warum halten wir uns Haustiere?
3. Was halten Sie von Zoos?

Transport
1. Vor- und Nachteile des Massentransports.
2. Was sind Ihrer Meinung nach die häufigsten Ursachen von Verkehrs-unfällen?
3. 'Fahren und Trinken – ein Selbstmordversuch'. Was halten Sie von dieser Behauptung?
4. 'Gib dem Menschen ein Lenkrad und es ist eine Einladung zur Persön-lichkeitsänderung!' Stimmt das?